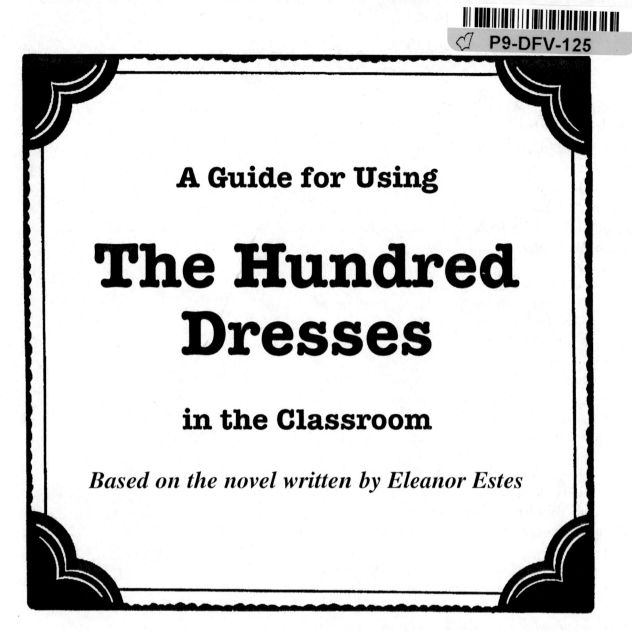

A Guide for Using

The Hundred Dresses

in the Classroom

Based on the novel written by Eleanor Estes

*This guide written by **Shelle Renae Allen-Russell***

Teacher Created Resources, Inc.
6421 Industry Way
Westminster, CA 92683
www.teachercreated.com
ISBN: 978-1-57690-136-6
© *1998 Teacher Created Resources, Inc.*
Reprinted, 2011
Made in U.S.A.

Edited by
Mary Kaye Taggart

Illustrated by
Larry Bauer

Cover Art by
Wendy Chang

Table of Contents

Introduction

An interesting book can create new ways to view the events in our lives. Inside its pages are words and characters which can teach us lessons and inspire us to become better people. We can read for enjoyment, knowledge, and guidance. The words found on the pages of books can impact our lives forever.

In *Literature Units*, great care has been taken to select books that are sure to be good friends!

Teachers who use this literature unit will find the following features to supplement their own valuable ideas.

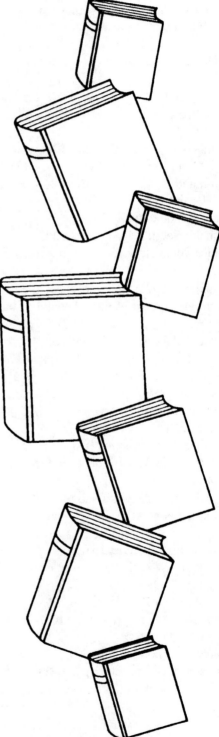

- Sample Lesson Plan

- Pre-reading Activities

- Biographical Sketch and Picture of the Author

- Book Summary

- Vocabulary Lists and Vocabulary Activity Ideas

- Chapters grouped for study with each section including some of the following:

    —*quizzes*

    —*hands-on projects*

    —*cross-curricular activities*

    —*cooperative learning activities*

    —*extensions into the reader's own life*

- Post-reading Activities

- Book Report Ideas

- Research Ideas

- Culminating Activities

- Three Unit Test Options

- Bibliography of Related Reading

- Answer Key

We are confident that this unit will be a valuable addition to your lesson planning. Through the use of our ideas, we hope that your students will increase the circle of "friends" they have in books.

Sample Lesson Plan

Each of the lessons suggested below can take from one to several days to complete.

Lesson 1
- Introduce and complete some of the pre-reading activities (page 5).
- Decorate your room with the dresses and motorboats from the contest (page 6).
- Read About the Author with your students (page 7).
- Introduce the vocabulary list for Section 1 (page 9).

Lesson 2
- Read chapter 1. As you read, place the vocabulary words in the context of the story and discuss their meanings.
- Do a vocabulary activity (page 10).
- Make a Compliment Sandwich (page 12).
- Work on and complete the Map Skills activity (pages 13 and 14).
- Begin scrapbooks (page 15).
- Administer Section 1 quiz (page 11).
- Introduce vocabulary for Section 2 (page 9).

Lesson 3
- Read chapter 2. As you read, place the vocabulary words in the context of the story and discuss their meanings.
- Do a vocabulary activity (page 10).
- Solve the Soupy Math problems (page 17).
- Assign Subject and Predicate Mania (pages 18 and 19).
- Plan a Clothing Drive (page 20).
- Continue scrapbooks (page 15).
- Administer Section 2 quiz (page 16).
- Introduce vocabulary for Section 3 (page 9).

Lesson 4
- Read chapter 3. As you read, place the vocabulary words in the context of the story and discuss their meanings.
- Do a vocabulary activity (page 10).
- Complete the What Is the Score? math activity (page 22).
- Try some Polish Recipes (page 23).
- Discuss and analyze peer pressure in the students' lives (page 24).
- Continue scrapbooks (page 15).
- Administer Section 3 quiz (page 21).
- Introduce vocabulary list for Section 4 (page 9).

Lesson 5
- Read chapter 4. As you read, place the vocabulary words in the context of the story and discuss their meanings.
- Do a vocabulary activity (page 10).
- Practice Choral Reading in groups (page 26).
- Do the Adjectives and Adverbs activity (page 27).
- Make boats and race them (pages 28 and 29).
- Continue scrapbooks (page 15).
- Administer Section 4 quiz (page 25).
- Introduce vocabulary for Section 5 (page 9).

Lesson 6
- Read chapter 5. As you read, place the vocabulary words in the context of the story and discuss their meanings.
- Do a vocabulary activity (page 10).
- Find the Hidden Objects (pages 31 and 32).
- Design New Desks (page 33).
- Write personal letters to Miss Mason (page 34).
- Continue scrapbooks (page 15).
- Administer Section 5 quiz (page 30).
- Introduce vocabulary for Section 6 (page 9).

Lesson 7
- Read chapters 6 and 7. As you read, place the vocabulary words in the context of the story and discuss their meanings.
- Do a vocabulary activity (page 10).
- Discuss and complete Immigration Booms! (page 36).
- Discuss and graph the dresses from the classroom contest (page 37).
- Ask the students to investigate their family trees (page 38).
- Complete scrapbooks (page 15).
- Administer Section 6 quiz (page 35).

Lesson 8
- Discuss any questions or comments the students may have about the book (page 39).
- Assign book reports and research activities (pages 40 and 41).
- Begin work on a culminating activity (page 42).

Lesson 9
- Administer Unit Test Options 1, 2, and/or 3 (pages 43–45).
- Discuss the test answers and responses.
- Discuss the students' opinions and enjoyment of the book.
- Complete a culminating activity.
- Provide the students with a list of related reading.

Before the Book

Before you begin reading *The Hundred Dresses* with your students, do some activities to stimulate their interest and enhance their comprehension. Here are some activities which may work for your students.

1. Ask the students to make word search puzzles from the vocabulary words.

2. Predict what the story might be about by hearing the title.

3. Predict what the story might be about by looking at the cover illustrations.

4. Discuss peer pressure. Challenge the students to make up short skits showing the students in peer pressure situations similar to those in the book but with different outcomes. For example, the students might do a skit about teasing someone because he or she is not good in sports. Two different outcomes for this situation might be . . .

   . . . the student is mistreated and made fun of by the others.

   . . . the student is supported by one or more of the others.

5. Divide the students into groups to find articles in the local or area newspapers in which people have been helped by others. Ask the groups to share the articles that they discovered and what the outcomes were.

6. Ask the students to draw comic strips or pictures showing how people can help those who are different from them.

7. Talk about classroom, town, and national rules which concern the treatment of others. Discuss the following questions:

   • Why are rules made?

   • What good things happen because of rules?

   • Can you think of any rules that help others make their choices?

   • If there were no guidelines for how to treat others, what would happen in our society?

   • If a person chooses to continue to ignore the rules of the classroom, school, or society, how might his or her decisions affect the lives of others?

8. Have a class contest similar to the one in the book. Give each student two entry forms (page 6). The students may enter in either or both categories: dresses or motorboats. The entry forms should each have the category of choice circled. Set guidelines for the students or let them use any medium they wish for the contest: marker, crayon, pencil, watercolor, construction paper, etc.

   Display the motorboats in one area of the classroom and the dresses in another. Ask other teachers to help you choose the best entries. Award prizes to the first-, second-, and third-place winners of the contest. Prizes may be awarded for categories such as most interesting design or most eye-catching.

Before the Book *(cont.)*

Classroom Contest

Directions: Choose a category, dresses or motorboats, and circle your choice below. Create a picture for your chosen category on this entry form. Concentrate on being creative!

Name: _____   Date: _____

Category: **dresses**   **motorboats**

About the Author

Eleanor Estes was born to Louis and Caroline Rosefield on May 9, 1906, in the town of West Haven, Connecticut. She attended elementary and high school in New Haven.

After high school, Eleanor began working for the children's department at the New Haven Free Public Library. In 1928 she became the head librarian. Soon after, she received the Caroline M. Hewin Scholarship for Children's Librarians and went to New York to study at the Pratt Institute Library School.

Upon entering Pratt, Eleanor met Rice Estes. They were married shortly after. Eleanor worked at the New York Public Library until 1941 when she published her first book, *The Moffats*. Eleanor published nine books in all. She enjoyed writing, drawing, painting, and taking walks by the ocean. She died in 1988.

Eleanor Estes also wrote the following books:

When asked about her writing, Eleanor Estes once said:

"In my writing I like to feel that I am holding up a mirror, and I hope that what is reflected is a true image of childhood and echoes the clear, profound, and unpremeditated thoughts and imageries of childhood. I like to make children laugh or cry, or move them in some way. I am happy that my books have been translated into many languages, and I am grateful to the children everywhere who have looked in my mirror and liked what they have seen." (*The Junior Book of Authors,* Second Revised Edition. New York, H. W. Wilson Co., 1951.)

The Hundred Dresses

by Eleanor Estes

(Harcourt Brace and Company, 1944)

(Available in Canada and UK, HBJ; AUS, HBJ Aus.)

The Hundred Dresses takes place in a small town mainly composed of people who have lived in the United States for long periods of time. An immigrant family moves into the community from another country. The family has very little money and lives in a rundown but affordable section of town.

The immigrant family has many hard times and is struggling to survive in a new country. The mother has died, and the father is attempting to raise his son and daughter alone. He is aware of the needs of his children and understands their struggles. He loves his children dearly and only wants them to be treated fairly, regardless of their nationality, unusual last name, or clothing.

The main characters are Wanda, Peggy, and Maddie. Each girl is quite different in personality, behavior, and looks.

Wanda is the Polish girl who has just immigrated to the United States with her father and brother. Each day she wears the same faded blue dress because it is the only one she owns. She is a very kind little girl who desperately desires to fit in. She notices many things about all of the children in class, especially Peggy and Maddie, the popular ones. She tries to gain their acceptance by making up stories. This causes the other children to ridicule her on a daily basis.

Peggy is the most popular girl in the class. She is often extremely self-righteous. Peggy is from a middle- to upper-class family and always has new clothing. She is controlling, and she hurts students who are different from her. She continually justifies her behavior to herself and others.

Maddie, on the other hand, is from a lower income family, much like Wanda is. However, she and Peggy have been best friends for a long time. Her clothes are hand-me-downs from Peggy, which her mother has altered and trimmed. Maddie thinks a great deal about how others feel, but for the majority of the book she does not have the courage it takes to stand up to Peggy. In the end, Maddie realizes that by allowing the ridicule and teasing to continue, she is just as much at fault as Peggy and the others are.

The story centers around the children's game with Wanda. They tease her because she says she has a hundred dresses. Wanda's desire to fit in only brings her ridicule as the children focus on her outer appearance (her faded blue dress) instead of her inner qualities.

The Hundred Dresses concludes with Wanda and her family moving to a large city where her father feels that their cultural differences will be less obvious. He feels that his children might fit in better in the city. The teacher from the small town feels sad to think that her students may have been part of the reason for the move, and she talks to them about being unfair. Maddie decides that she can no longer treat a person unfairly because of his or her outer appearance or nationality. She promises to change her behavior if she is faced with a similar situation again.

Vocabulary Lists

On this page are vocabulary lists which correspond to each section as outlined in the table of contents. Vocabulary activity ideas can be found on page 10 of this book.

Section 1: *Chapter 1*

absence	entertainment
askew	precarious
caked	roars
contrary	scuffling
crooked	twisted

Section 2: *Chapter 2*

broad	intruders
circulated	peals
disgracefully	safely
furthermore	scurry
incredulously	strewn

Section 3: *Chapter 3*

flashed	slightest
hesitate	stolidly
impatiently	swiftly
particular	vaguest
puckered	vividly

Section 4: *Chapter 4*

admiration	paused
announce	recognize
brilliant	shuddered
consisted	timid
disguise	uncomfortable

Section 5: *Chapter 5*

admiringly	lavish
dazzling	murmured
deliberately	spread
dismissed	submitted
gasped	whistled

Section 6: *Chapters 6 and 7*

ashamed	intently
blurred	relieve
dilapidated	rickety
finality	sparse
forbidding	vanished

Vocabulary Activity Ideas

You can help your students learn and retain the vocabulary in *The Hundred Dresses* by providing them with interesting vocabulary activities. Here are some ideas to try.

- ❑ **Word searches** and **crossword puzzles** are enjoyable for all ages. Your students can use vocabulary words from the story to create crossword and/or word search puzzles individually or in teams.

- ❑ Encourage the **usage** of the vocabulary words! Writing sentences is a very good way to expand usage. Encourage the students to write in themes such as silly or ridiculous sentences, animal sentences, people sentences, or serious sentences. Then ask for volunteers to share some of their sentences out loud.

- ❑ **Vocabulary shapes** can be interesting. Have the students select several vocabulary words from each chapter. Ask them to lightly draw shapes (in pencil) that remind them of the words. Next, tell them to write the words around the edges of the shapes as many times as they can in marker, crayon, or colored pencil. This is an excellent activity for the students to do in their free time. It also makes a creative and attractive bulletin board.

- ❑ Create a **vocabulary game**. Give each group of three students 70 pieces of 3" x 5" (7.6 cm x 12.7 cm) paper. On the papers, have the students write each consonant in the alphabet two times and each vowel three times. After they have completed the letters, have them organize the papers into stacks on their desks. Begin the game by calling out a vocabulary word or the definition of one of the vocabulary words. Challenge the groups to use their cards to cooperatively spell the word correctly on their desks. Do not allow talking, whispering, or sharing answers. As a team finishes spelling the word, one member should raise a thumb. Quickly check the work of the finished teams and push down the thumbs of those who misspelled the word. Give a point to each team that spelled the word correctly and an extra point to the team that was the first to finish. Record the teams' points on the board. This is a quiet, exciting, interactive game.

- ❑ Have the students **advertise** their vocabulary words in groups or individually. Give each student (or group of students) a large sheet of paper. Ask them to try to "sell" their vocabulary words by creating advertisements. Share their finished products with the class. Posters should include words, costs, the benefits of each word, etc.

- ❑ Play **Vocabulary Concentration**. The goal of this game is to match vocabulary words with their definitions. Divide the class into groups of two to five students. Have the students make two sets of cards the same size and color. On one set, have them write the vocabulary words. On the second set, have students write the definitions. All cards are mixed together and placed face down on a table. A player chooses two cards. If the pair matches the word with its definition, the player keeps the cards and takes another turn. If the cards do not match, they are returned to their places facedown on the table, and another player takes a turn. Players must concentrate to remember the locations of words and definitions. The game continues until all matches have been made. This is an ideal activity for free exploration time.

You probably have many more ideas to add to this list. Try them! Practicing selected words through these types of activities increases student interest in, and retention of, vocabulary.

Quiz Time

Directions: Answer the questions using complete sentences. Use the back of this paper if you need more room.

1. Describe Wanda. How does she look and act?

   _____

   _____

2. How do the other kids feel about Wanda? How do we know?

   _____

   _____

3. Describe Peggy. How does she dress and act?

   _____

   _____

4. Why do Peggy and Maddie (finally) notice Wanda is absent?

   _____

   _____

5. Where does Wanda sit in the classroom? Why do you think she sits there?

   _____

   _____

6. What are the kids like who sit in the same part of the room as Wanda?

   _____

   _____

7. What does the teacher have the children recite each morning?

   _____

   _____

8. How is Wanda different from the other students?

   _____

   _____

Compliment Sandwich

Teacher Directions: Divide the students into pairs for this exercise. Give each student a copy of this page.

Directions: Spend some time with your partner discussing things that you have in common and things that make you unique. Then, spend a few minutes filling in the compliment sandwich about your partner. Try to concentrate on positive comments about the real person and not his or her outward appearance. When you are both finished, exchange, read, and discuss the sandwiches.

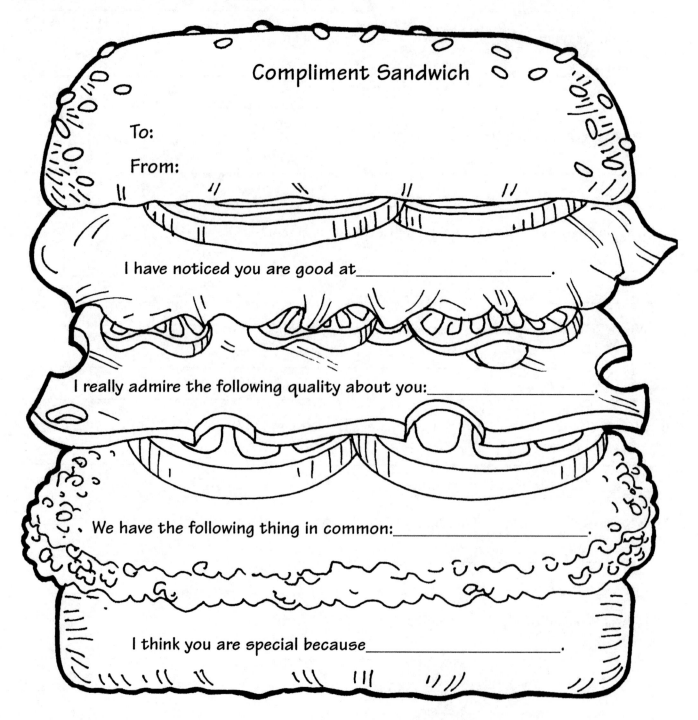

Compliment Sandwich

To:

From:

I have noticed you are good at_____.

I really admire the following quality about you:_____.

We have the following thing in common:_____.

I think you are special because_____.

Map Skills

Directions: Below is an imaginary map of what Maddie's and Peggy's town may look like. Look at the map carefully and answer the questions which follow.

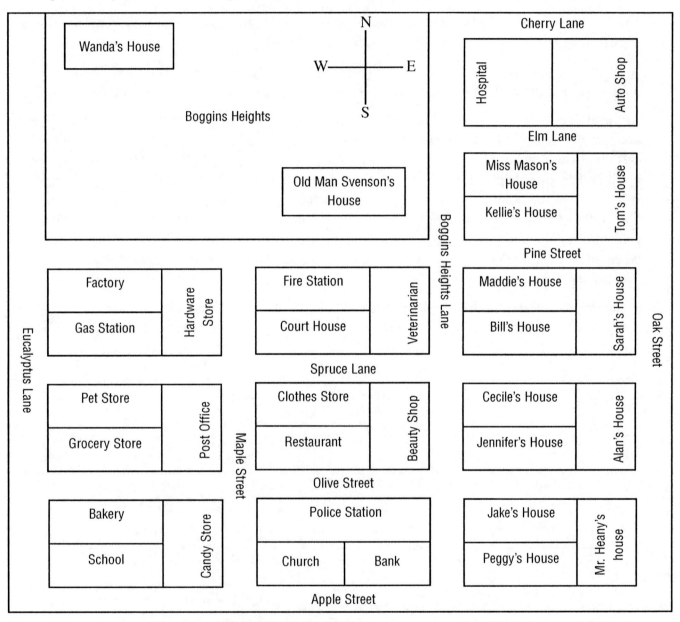

1. Leave Maddie's house on Pine Street and head west. Turn south on Maple Street. Walk three blocks and look to your right. What is the last thing that you see on this street on your right?

2. What is the quickest way to get to school from Wanda's house?

3. There is a criminal who has just robbed the auto shop. The nearest police car is at the corner of Eucalyptus Lane and Apple Street. What is the fastest way for him to get to the auto shop? Name the streets in the correct order.

Map Skills *(cont.)*

4. One day Bill is very late for school because he oversleeps. He has to stop by Tom's house to pick him up. What is one of the fastest ways they can get to school from Tom's house?

5. The fire fighters from the fire station have to get someone to the hospital quickly. The fire was at Mr. Heany's house. Name two quick routes to the hospital.

6. After school, several of the boys wanted to take the long way home. Carefully follow the directions, and list each of the places at which they stopped before they reached home.

   All of the boys left school, walking east on Apple Street. Then they went north on Maple Street and stopped at the first store on the left. It was the_____. Next they turned east on Olive Street and stopped for a soda at the_____. After this, they went north on Boggins Heights Lane. They stopped at the second block that they came to and visited Bill's mom at the place where she worked. It was the_____. By that time it was getting late so they turned east and walked one block on Pine Street. They turned north on Oak and ended up at _____ house. Each boy called his parents and asked if he could stay for dinner. _____ mother had to make extra spaghetti that night because there were so many boys!

7. Write several questions of your own to correspond with the map. Make them interesting. Use north, south, east, and west in your questions. If you need more writing space, use the back of this paper.

   _____

   _____

   _____

   _____

   _____

   _____

Extension: On a separate piece of paper, draw a map of the way you think the town in *The Hundred Dresses* might look. Write five or more questions that can be answered using your map. Remember to use the directions north, south, east, and west in the questions. Trade maps with a classmate and answer each other's questions.

Scrapbooks

One great way to remember what you read in *The Hundred Dresses* is to make a scrapbook with one page for each chapter. To make it more interesting, write your summaries for each chapter from the perspective of one of the characters in the book. For example, you may want to create a scrapbook from Peggy's point of view—as if she were writing it herself.

Choose one of the following characters to speak through for your scrapbook.

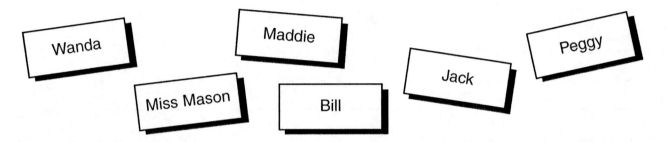

After you choose your character, look for clues in the book about his or her personality. If you cannot find much information about your character's personality, create some personality traits for him or her. As you write, consider how your character might retell the events and how he or she might react to them. If you choose to become a character who is not in every scene, you will have to summarize some chapters as if you heard about the events from someone else.

To make your scrapbook, carefully follow the directions below.

1. Fold five pieces of 8 ¹/₂" x 11" (22 cm x 28 cm) paper in half to make an 8¹/₂" x 5¹/₂" (22 cm x 14 cm) book. Staple the pieces together along the center.

2. Design a cover for your scrapbook. On the cover write a title for the scrapbook, and at the bottom print your name.

3. Make the second page a title page. Include the name of the scrapbook, your name, and the name of the character you will be portraying on the right side.

4. Turn the page. Draw a large rectangle on the left side. Draw and color a picture from the first chapter in this rectangle.

5. On the right side of the page, neatly print the title of the first chapter at the top. Then write a four- or five- sentence summary of the chapter from the perspective of your chosen character.

6. After you finish reading each chapter, make another entry in your scrapbook. Include a picture on the left side and the chapter title and summary on the right side.

7. After you have finished writing entries for all seven chapters, check your scrapbook for neatness, spelling, punctuation, and grammar. If you have an extra page or two at the end, you may want to make up your own final chapter. What will happen to your character in the future? What did your character learn from his or her experiences?

Quiz Time

Directions: Answer the questions using complete sentences. Use the back of this paper if you need more room.

1. Why do Peggy and Maddie feel like intruders in their own classroom at the beginning of this chapter?

   _____

   _____

2. What do Peggy and Maddie notice after they enter the classroom?

   _____

   _____

3. What game do the girls play regularly? What does this tell us about the kind of children they are?

   _____

   _____

4. What is Wanda's response to their game?

   _____

   _____

5. Where does Wanda stand to wait for the school bell to ring each day?

   _____

   _____

6. Chapter 2 tells us what Maddie really thinks about the treatment of Wanda. What does she think?

   _____

   _____

7. Have you ever seen this type of game being played before? Describe what you saw.

   _____

   _____

8. How would playing this game make you feel inside?

   _____

   _____

   _____

Soupy Math

Wanda may have eaten cabbage soup. It is a fairly inexpensive meal often eaten by people from poorer European countries. Below is a recipe for six people. Pretend that there are thirty people in your class and that you need to make enough soup for everyone. With your group try to decide how much of each ingredient you will need and how much each ingredient will cost. When you have finished, add up the ingredient prices to figure out the total cost of feeding all thirty students. (**Teacher Note:** If using metric measurements, convert ingredients to metrics first.)

Ingredients

Serves 6	Cost for 6	Workspace	Cost for 30
1 small green cabbage	69¢		
2 slices of bacon	20¢		
1 large onion, chopped	49¢		
2 small leeks (white part only), sliced	50¢		
2 carrots, sliced	24¢		
1 potato, sliced	50¢		
1 tablespoon of flour	2¢		
4 cups of brown stock	59¢		
2 tablespoons of parsley, chopped	40¢		
1 bay leaf	10¢		
a pinch of nutmeg	2¢		
1 teaspoon of dill seeds	30¢		
4 frankfurters, fried and sliced	64¢		
fat for frying	20¢		

Total Cost _____

Subject and Predicate Mania

Learning grammar can be fun. To be successful you need to learn the basics. Read the explanations of a subject and a predicate.

A **subject** is a word that tells what or who the sentence is about.

Here is an example:

A young, petite **girl** ran slowly down the path to Boggins Heights.

A **predicate** is the part of a sentence which shows the action of the subject or says something about the subject.

Here is an example:

The tiny, green turtle **waddled** lazily toward the brown rock.

Look at each of the sentences below. Use a **yellow** crayon or marker to underline the **subject** in each sentence. Use a green crayon or marker to underline the **predicate** in each sentence.

1. Peggy would not stop teasing Wanda.

2. All students submitted entries.

3. Maddie sharpened her pencil slowly and deliberately.

4. Maddie and Cecile joined the group.

5. They stopped and gasped.

6. A slight frown puckered her forehead.

7. Their sweaters caught the sun's rays.

8. A crisp, angry wind swished their skirts.

9. Each student did artwork for the contest.

10. Wanda's class applauded.

11. Miss Mason clapped her hands and stomped her feet.

12. Bill shuffled his feet.

Bonus: Write three of your own sentences about *The Hundred Dresses* on the back of this paper. Stick closely to the ideas and characters in the book. Use your crayons or markers to underline the subjects and predicates.

Subject and Predicate Mania *(cont.)*

Now that we know how to find subjects (nouns) and predicates (verbs), we need to learn how to find complete subjects and complete predicates.

<table>
<tr>
<td>

A **complete subject** includes who or what the sentence is about and any words that describe the subject, usually adjectives.

Example: The tiny mouse . . .

</td>
<td>

A **complete predicate** involves the action or state of being, as well as words which describe the verb, usually adverbs. It may include other words as well.

Example: . . . wandered slowly down a dark hallway.

</td>
</tr>
</table>

Look at the sentences below. Draw a line to separate the complete subject of each sentence from its complete predicate.

Example: The small, frail boy **/** glanced timidly at Peggy on the playground.
          complete subject   *complete predicate*

1. Maddie stumbled on the wet patch of earth.

2. Thoughts of Wanda floated through her mind slowly.

3. The following day was extremely drizzly and cold.

4. Many excited students stared at the colorful dresses.

5. Several light blue clouds moved gently across the sky.

6. Both boys burst out laughing loudly.

7. Wanda silently entered the empty classroom.

8. Maddie's desk slammed shut with a bang.

9. Big Bill Byron placed his large, muddy feet on Wanda's chair.

10. Wanda was absent from school.

11. The two most popular students, Peggy and Maddie, noticed Wanda was not in school.

12. Several children chose to color their boats green.

Bonus: Write three of your own sentences about *The Hundred Dresses* on the back of this paper. Stick closely to the ideas and characters in the book. Draw lines to divide the complete subjects from the complete predicates.

Clothing Drive

Note to the Teacher: In the second chapter we learn more about Wanda's background. She comes from a poor immigrant family, and she does not own much clothing. The author explains that Wanda wears the same tired dress to school every day. Unfortunately, her lack of a larger wardrobe is one of the things that keeps Wanda from fitting in.

The following activity will help your students recognize that it is unfair to judge people by how they look. It will also teach them the importance of helping others.

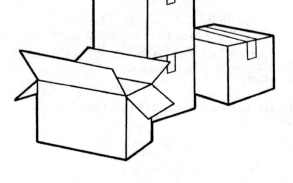

Materials:

- boxes in which to organize and package clothing
- black markers to mark the boxes
- letters to the parents explaining the clothing drive

Directions:

1. Lead a discussion with your students about how it would feel to be in Wanda's situation. What would it be like to have to wear the same outfit to school every day? How would you be treated? What does a person's clothing actually say about the real person? Is it fair to choose friends on the basis of wardrobe alone? (**Note:** Before initiating this discussion, consider the actual financial situations of your students. If portions of this discussion might make some of your students uncomfortable, make the necessary adjustments.)

2. Explain to your students what a clothing drive is and ask them to help you plan one.

3. Brainstorm a list of charities that might want to receive the clothing donations. (**Note:** Try to lead the suggestions away from the shelters, homes, or other organizations that might include people who are students at your school. It could be uncomfortable if a student showed up at school in clothing donated by one of his or her classmates.) Vote on a charity choice, and then call the charity and see if they would like to receive the donation.

4. Decide on a date.

5. Determine if you would like to make this a schoolwide event or a class activity. If you do choose to make the activity schoolwide, notify the other teachers and the principal of your plans.

6. Write a letter home to explain the activity to the parents. Ask them to search through their own and their children's closets to look for any clothing that no longer fits or is no longer wanted. Request that all of the donations be recently laundered, and ask the parents to thoroughly check all of the pockets for personal possessions. Give any other details such as the date of the drive, the receiving charity, and drop-off information.

7. Let the students receive and package, in boxes, the donations as they come in. They may wish to organize the contents of the boxes by size, gender, type of garment, etc. Ask them to label the boxes with markers.

8. When the boxes are ready, deliver the clothing!

Quiz Time

Directions: Answer the questions using complete sentences. Use the back of this paper if you need more room.

1. Why is Maddie unable to concentrate on her school work?

   _____

   _____

2. When did the game originally begin?

   _____

   _____

3. "For now Peggy seemed to think the day was lost if she had not had some fun with Wanda." What does this sentence mean? What do you think it tells us about Peggy?

   _____

   _____

4. Why do you think Wanda chose to tell Peggy that she has a hundred dresses?

   _____

   _____

5. What does Peggy do with the information she receives from Wanda?

   _____

   _____

6. How does Wanda respond to the teasing?

   _____

   _____

7. Who else becomes involved in Peggy's game?

   _____

   _____

8. Think back to Maddie as she sat on the curb before the game started. Describe what she might have been thinking.

   _____

   _____

What Is the Score?

Teacher Directions: Use these story problems to create an exciting math game. Divide the class into cooperative groups. Give each group a copy of this page. Call out the story problem numbers, one at a time, for the groups to solve. Have a competition to see which group can get the most correct answers. Keep track of the scores on the board.

+   **−**

1. If Wanda draws five dresses each day, how many days would it take for her to draw all 100 dresses?

2. If Peggy has 60 pairs of shoes and she wears two pairs each day, how many days would it take for her to wear each pair once?

3. In Wanda's school there are seven classes, one for each grade. If there are 32 students per class, how many students are in the school?

4. If every student in one class has one eraser, one textbook, and two pencils for science class, how many pencils would there be for the entire class (32 students)?

5. In Bill's classroom they need 32 desks, but they only have 26. How many do they still need?

6. If Miss Mason plans to give each student three pieces of paper for art, how many pieces does she need to bring to class for her 32 students?

7. If each one of Miss Mason's 32 students designs two boats, how many designs would the class have?

8. Each student (in a class of 32 students) bought four pencils at the pencil machine. Pencils cost 25 cents for two. How much money did the entire class spend for the pencils they purchased?

9. On a drizzly, rainy day, everyone was having a hard time concentrating. If each of the 32 students glanced out the window five times, how many glances were there in all?

10. If Maddie has to walk five blocks to school and five blocks home, how many blocks does she have to walk in one week?

÷   **X**

Polish Recipes

Maddie and Peggy did not have a chance to try Polish food because they did not take the time to get to know Wanda. However, there are many Polish foods that taste very good.

Tasting food from other lands and cultures is one of the interesting things that you can experience when you make friends with people from different backgrounds. Below are two recipes Wanda may have learned to cook as a little girl or when she grew up. If you make them at home, remember to ask your parents for permission before you begin. Also, you may wish to ask someone to help you with the recipes. (**Note:** If using metric measurements, convert ingredients to metrics first.)

━━━━━ Polish Easter Cake (*serves eight*) ━━━━━

Ingredients:

- $\frac{1}{2}$ cup flour
- $\frac{1}{2}$ cup granulated sugar
- $\frac{1}{2}$ teaspoon salt
- $\frac{1}{2}$ cup raisins
- 1 cup confectioners' sugar

- $\frac{1}{4}$ cup butter
- $\frac{1}{4}$ cup warm water
- 1 package active yeast
- $\frac{1}{2}$ cup milk
- $\frac{1}{2}$ teaspoon grated lemon peel

- 2 eggs, beaten
- 2 $\frac{1}{2}$ cups flour
- $\frac{1}{2}$ cup chopped almonds
- 1 tablespoon milk
- whole, candied cherries

Directions:

- Scald $\frac{1}{2}$ cup milk. Stir in the sugar, salt, and butter. Cool to lukewarm.
- Pour lukewarm water into large bowl. Sprinkle yeast over the water; stir until dissolved. Add the milk mixture, eggs, and flour; beat vigorously for five minutes. Cover. Let rise in a warm place, free from cool air, for 1 $\frac{1}{2}$ hours or until dough doubles in size.
- Stir down batter; beat in the almonds, raisins, and lemon peel. Pour the batter into a greased and floured deep cake pan. Let the batter rise one hour.
- Bake at 350° F (177° C) in the oven for 50 minutes. Let cool in the pan 20 minutes.
- Beat together confectioners' sugar and one tablespoon of milk to form a glaze.
- Place the cake on a serving platter, and drizzle the glaze on top. Garnish with a few cherries.

━━━━━ Polish Eggs in a Shell (*serves four*) ━━━━━

Ingredients:

- 4 hard-boiled eggs in shells
- 3 tablespoons butter
- 1 teaspoon paprika

- $\frac{1}{2}$ bunch parsley, finely chopped
- 1 teaspoon salt
- $\frac{1}{4}$ cup shredded Muenster cheese

Directions:

- Ask an adult to cut the eggs in half with a large, sharp knife.
- Scoop the eggs out of the shells very carefully. Thoroughly clean and dry the egg shells, and then set them aside.
- Finely chop the egg whites. Mash the yolks with a fork. Combine the chopped egg whites, mashed yolks, parsley, butter, salt, and paprika. Mix well.
- Refill the egg shells with the egg mixture and sprinkle with cheese.
- Bake for ten minutes at 400° F (204° C) or until the cheese melts and browns. Serve.

Peer Pressure

Your *peer* is someone who is your equal. This may mean that you share the same age or that you are in the same group or have the same status level. When you are a student, your peers are your classmates. Your teacher's peers are the other teachers in the school. People sometimes do things with their peers that they would never do alone. If your *peers pressure* you to do something, it is called peer pressure.

Other people can influence our actions by using peer pressure. Peer pressure is often a negative (or bad) thing. For example, if your peers talk you into stealing something, this is obviously negative peer pressure. However, peer pressure can sometimes be a positive (or good) thing. For example, if your class is offered a reward if everyone gets a perfect score on his or her spelling quizzes, and your classmates pressure you to study, this would be positive peer pressure.

1. What peer pressure does Maddie feel in *The Hundred Dresses*? _____

   _____

   _____

   Who pressures Maddie, and is it a positive or negative type of peer pressure? _____

   _____

2. Describe a time when you were involved in a negative peer pressure situation. _____

   _____

   _____

   How did this situation make you feel? _____

   Would you have acted any differently in this situation if there had not been any peer pressure involved? _____

3. Describe a time when you were involved in a positive peer pressure situation._____

   _____

   _____

   How did this situation make you feel? _____

   Would you have acted any differently in this situation if there had not been any peer pressure involved? _____

4. If you were in Maddie's situation, what would you do? _____

   _____

   _____

Quiz Time

Directions: Answer the questions using complete sentences. Use the back of this paper if you need more room.

1. What does Maddie consider writing to Peggy about? Why does she decide that it is not a good idea?

2. What are the boys supposed to draw for the classroom contest?

3. What are the girls supposed to draw for the classroom contest?

4. Maddie is sure that she knows who the winner is already. Who does she think is going to win?

5. In thinking about the contest, Maddie forgets all about one person. Who does she forget?

6. Why do you think Wanda has a difficult time reading?

7. Why do you think the other children are not willing to stand up to Peggy?

8. Why do you think it is so important for the children to feel accepted by Peggy?

Choral Reading

Choral reading can be fun! It happens when a group of several people read the same passage at the same time. Groups can be as small as two readers or as large as hundreds of readers. Below is the Gettysburg Address. Abraham Lincoln wrote this speech and delivered it at the dedication of a military cemetery. Each morning the students in Miss Mason's class recited it by heart. Instead of memorizing it, try reading it chorally. Here are some reading suggestions:

1. Separate into groups of two to four people and take turns reading the parts.
2. Divide into a girl group and a boy group. Switch the reading back and forth between the groups.
3. Have several readers read one part and then the entire class read the next part.
4. Create your own choral reading groups.

One thing to remember is to use your voices like a chorus to create feeling and enthusiasm. Choral reading is supposed to be enjoyable, not dull.

Gettysburg Address

Reader: Four score and seven years ago our fathers brought forth on this continent, a new nation, conceived in Liberty, and dedicated to the proposition that all men are created equal.

Reader: Now we are engaged in a great civil war, testing whether that nation, or any nation so conceived and so dedicated, can long endure. We are met on a great battlefield of that war. We have come to dedicate a portion of that field, as a final resting place for those who here gave their lives that that nation might live. It is altogether fitting and proper that we should do this.

Reader: But, in a larger sense, we can not dedicate—we can not consecrate—we can not hallow—this ground. The brave men, living and dead, who struggled here, have consecrated it, far above our poor power to add or detract. The world will little note, nor long remember what we say here, but it can never forget what they did here.

Reader: It is for us the living, rather, to be dedicated here to the unfinished work which they who fought here have thus far so nobly advanced. It is rather for us to be here dedicated to the great task remaining before us—that from these honored dead we take increased devotion to that cause for which they gave the last full measure of devotion—that we here highly resolve that these dead shall not have died in vain—

All Readers: —that this nation, under God, shall have a new birth of freedom—and that government of the people, by the people, for the people, shall not perish from the earth.

Abraham Lincoln

November 19, 1863

Adjectives and Adverbs

Now that you have reviewed subjects and predicates, let's move on to the words that describe each of them.

Adjectives modify or describe <u>nouns</u>. There is often more than one adjective for each noun.

    Example: The <u>small</u> man ran.

Adverbs modify or describe <u>verbs</u>. Adverbs describe how. Often, but not always, adverbs end in -ly.

    Example: The small man ran <u>slowly</u>.

Below are sentences about the characters and setting of *The Hundred Dresses*. Draw a circle around each adjective and a square around each adverb.

1. The tiny girl swung slowly.

2. A happy child looked at Wanda curiously.

3. Silly Peggy spoke quietly.

4. Grumpy Maddie thought angrily.

5. The excited children ran wildly and loudly.

6. Seven desks squeaked noisily.

7. Rambunctious boys climbed breathlessly.

8. Young Wanda dressed neatly.

9. The kind teacher smiled patiently.

10. Old Mr. Svenson worked fast and hard.

11. Wise Mr. Petronski sadly wrote a letter.

12. The thoughtless children carelessly teased Wanda.

Bonus: On the back of this paper, write five sentences of your own about the people and/or events in the story. Include adjectives and adverbs in each sentence. Circle the adjectives and draw a square around each of the adverbs.

What a Boat!

In *The Hundred Dresses*, the boys entered a drawing contest with a motorboat theme. Today, both boys and girls enjoy motorboats in the summer and sometimes, in warmer climates, throughout the year.

With your cooperative group, create four of your own boats by following the directions below. Then test the boats to see how quickly they can move.

Materials for Each Group:

- one or two file folders or pieces of cardboard
- a watch with a second hand
- a large plastic tub, $1/3$ to $1/2$ full of water
- two sheets of 8 $1/2$" x 11" (21.59 cm x 27.94 cm) aluminum foil
- two small milk cartons from the school cafeteria (Clean them with soap and hot water first.)
- scissors

Directions:

1. Cut around the bottom of one of the milk cartons, about a half inch (1.27 cm) up from the base. This will be the first boat.
2. Lay the other milk carton on its side and cut around the length of the carton, about a half inch (1.27 cm) up from the side. This will be the second boat.
3. Form two boats out of the sheets of aluminum foil. Mold them into two different shapes. These will be the third and fourth boats.
4. Before you test the speeds of the boats, predict which one you think will be the fastest and which one will be the slowest.
5. Place the boats in the water one at a time.
6. One person can use a watch to time how long the boat takes to reach the other side. Meanwhile, another person can wave a file folder or a piece of cardboard to create enough wind to push the boat.
7. Test and record the speed of each boat. Do your test three times for each one.
8. After you have finished the test, discuss the results.

Predictions:

Before you begin testing the boats, predict which one will be the fastest and which one will be the slowest. Give reasons to support your prediction. Write your responses on the back of this paper.

Boat Number	1st Test	2nd Test	3rd Test

Conclusion:

Which boat was the fastest? _____

We think it was the fastest because _____.

What a Boat! *(cont.)*

Now that you know which boat is the fastest, do some testing to learn which one can hold the most weight before sinking.

Materials for Each Group:
- the four boats made for the speed tests
- a large plastic tub, $^1\!/_3$ to $^1\!/_2$ full of water
- bottle caps

Directions:
1. Before you begin the testing, predict which boats will be the easiest and hardest to sink.
2. Place a boat in the water.
3. Have one person carefully load the boat with bottle caps while another person counts the number of caps.
4. Record the number of caps the boat can carry before it sinks.
5. Do this same test three times for each boat.

Predictions:

Before you begin testing, predict which boat will be the easiest to sink and which will be the hardest. Give reasons to support your predictions. Write your responses on the back of this paper.

Durability Test

Boat Number	1st Test	2nd Test	3rd Test

Conclusion:

Which boat was the easiest to sink?_____

We think it was the easiest boat to sink because _____

_____

_____.

Bonus:

Try using other objects to sink the boats. Are the results the same? Does changing the shape of the aluminum boats make a difference?

Quiz Time

Directions: Answer the questions using complete sentences. Use the back of this paper if you need more room.

1. At the start of the fifth chapter, the girls decide not to wait to make fun of Wanda that particular day. What are their two reasons?

    _____

    _____

2. Who is the winner of the girls' drawing contest, and what is so unusual about her entry?

    _____

    _____

3. Miss Mason receives a note from the principal. How does she react to it, and what comments does she make to her class?

    _____

    _____

4. How does the note make Maddie feel?

    _____

    _____

5. What question does Maddie remember Peggy repeatedly asking Wanda?

    _____

    _____

6. Why do you think the teacher could only display the girls' contest entries in room 13?

    _____

    _____

7. How has Maddie become just as much a part of the game as everyone else?

    _____

    _____

8. What does Peggy say that indicates she plans to cause problems for Wanda after school?

    _____

    _____

    _____

Hidden Objects

Look at the puzzle and color each part of speech the color listed in the box. When you are finished, the puzzle should reveal an object from *The Hundred Dresses*.

Nouns (Subjects)—blue	**Adjectives**—gray
Verbs (Predicates)—red	**Adverbs**—green

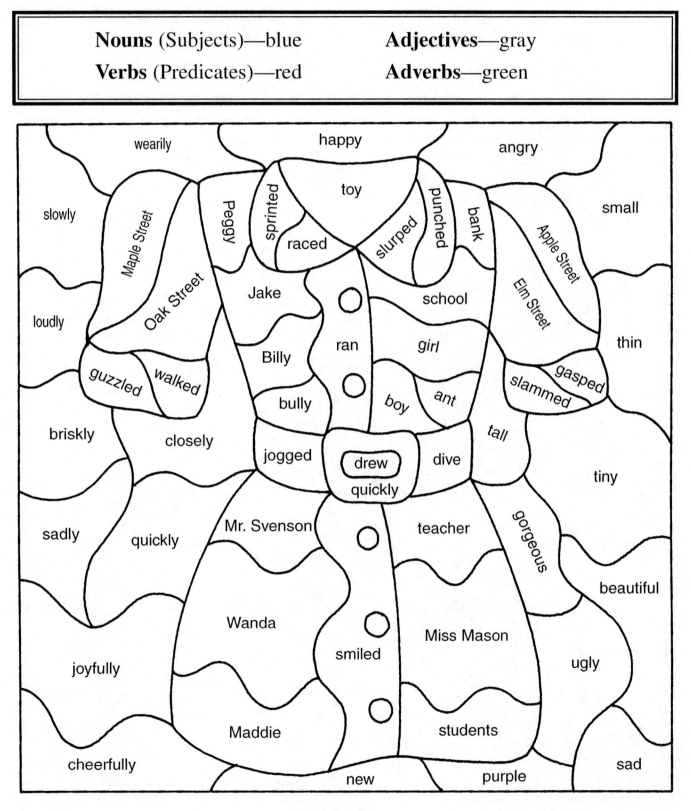

Hidden Objects *(cont.)*

Take another challenge. Look at the puzzle and color each part of speech the color listed in the box.
When you are finished, the puzzle should reveal another object from *The Hundred Dresses*.

Nouns (Subjects)—green	**Adjectives**—light blue
Verbs (Predicates)—dark blue	**Adverbs**—yellow

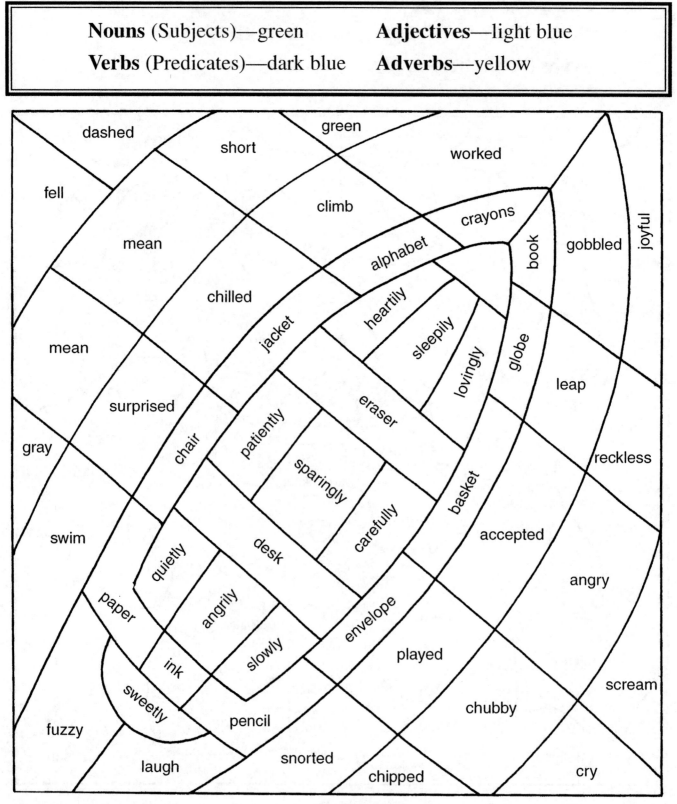

New Desks

The desks in Miss Mason's class were very, very old-fashioned. In the space below, design a desk which you feel would better serve students today. It can be as creative as you want it to be, but remember, it cannot be too large because classrooms have limited space. Your desk can have gadgets and other extra features. Label or write descriptions about the special features of your design.

Write On!

Pretend that you are in Wanda's class. Last week you joined in the game with all of the other children.

This morning Miss Mason got the letter from Wanda's father. She is one of your favorite teachers, and you can tell that she is very disappointed. You feel bad because you joined in and did not even think about Wanda's feelings. You are so angry with yourself that you make a promise to try harder to be nice to students who are not like you.

Write a letter to Miss Mason, explaining what you did to contribute to the problem and how you plan to act the next time someone is being teased. Divide your letter into two paragraphs.

    1st Paragraph: Describe the problem as you understand it and how you were involved.

    2nd Paragraph: Propose a solution to the problem if you are ever in a similar situation again.

Dear Miss Mason,

_____

_____

_____

_____

_____

_____

_____

_____

_____

                                         Sincerely,

                                    _____

Quiz Time

Directions: Answer the questions in complete sentences. Use the back of this paper if you need more room.

1. What is Boggins Heights like? Describe it.

   _____

   _____

2. What rumor had the two girls heard about Mr. Svenson?

   _____

   _____

3. Describe Wanda's house and yard.

   _____

   _____

4. How do Peggy and Maddie feel when no one is at Wanda's home?

   _____

   _____

5. What problem do Peggy and Maddie have when they want to mail their letter? What do they decide is their only hope?

   _____

   _____

6. How does Maddie treat Wanda differently in her dreams?

   _____

   _____

7. Why do you think Wanda says she has a hundred dresses?

   _____

   _____

8. What does Maddie understand about Wanda after hearing her letter? What does she notice about her picture?

   _____

   _____

Bonus: (Answer on the back of this paper.) What do you think Wanda is really trying to "say" through her drawings?

Immigration Booms!

Directions: With your cooperative learning group, read the following article on immigration. Discuss the questions as a group, and write the answers on a separate piece of paper. Then discuss the questions as a whole class.

Immigration

Someone who moves from one place to another to live permanently is called an *immigrant*. The United States is a country composed mainly of immigrants. People have moved to America for hundreds of years. They have come from many different countries and for a variety of reasons, such as to gain religious freedom, seek a better life, or escape bills and collection agencies. Still others have come to make money, escape poverty, or fulfill dreams. Today the United States has had to make laws about immigration because of the large number of people who entered in the past. It is not as easy to immigrate into the United States as it once was.

Immigrants of the past often faced many hardships after arriving in the United States. Some faced hardships such as a lack of jobs, discrimination and prejudice, unsanitary living conditions, poor housing, and crowded neighborhoods. Some of these conditions still remain today, especially in large cities with large populations of immigrants. Immigrants of the past and present have also experienced language barriers, little knowledge of different customs, and a different currency system.

Being an immigrant was never easy. Some came to the United States and became very successful. Others were hardly able to make a living. The situation is the same today for many immigrants; some succeed in the United States while others just get by.

Questions

1. How was life hard for those who immigrated to America?

2. How is being an immigrant a hardship in today's society?

3. How is it possible to create a more equal environment in the public schools despite the differences in family incomes?

4. Many schools have created a safer, more equal environment for all students. One idea has been to require uniforms for all students. Design a uniform which could be worn at your school to eliminate the obvious differences in family income.

Graph It

Teacher Directions: In this activity, the class will be graphing the dress drawings from the contest described on pages 5 and 6 of this book. Display the dresses for all of the students to see. Discuss the different ways the dresses could be categorized.

Divide the students into groups of two or three. Give each student a piece of graph paper. Give the groups enough time to choose four to five categories to divide the dresses into. Since there are many ways to divide and categorize, allow the students the freedom to experiment and evaluate. Help the students to set up their graphs. Tell them to list their categories horizontally along the bottom of the graph. Then they will list the numbers vertically along the side of the graph. Have them list as many numbers as there are drawings (for example, if there are 20 drawings, there should be 20 numbers along the side of the graph). Next, ask them to count the number of dresses that fit into each category. Have them graph the data. Share and discuss the graph results as a class.

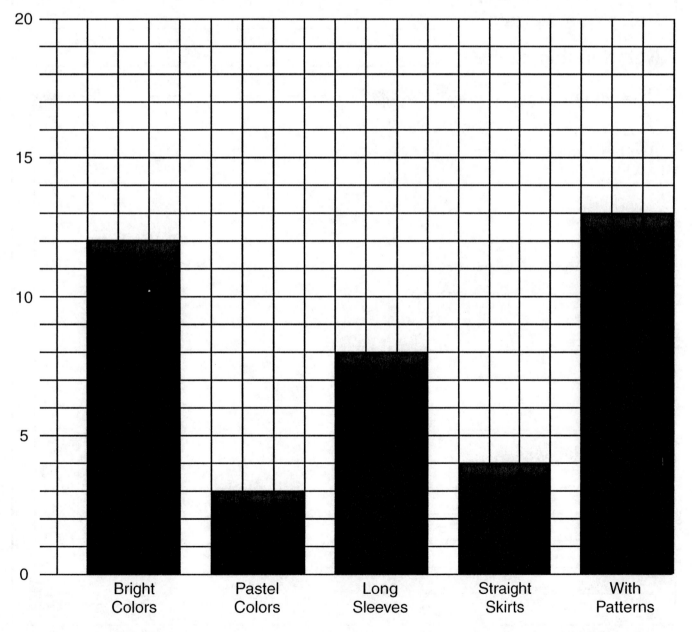

Check Your Roots

It is always interesting to learn information about our own families. Find out about your family and where your ancestors came from by talking to your relatives and researching any written family trees you might have. Record the data that you learn on a page for each individual family member. When you have finished, cut out the pages and staple them together to make your own family history book. If you know what each person looks or looked like, draw a picture of him or her also.

Try to fill out one page for each of the following relatives: mother, father, mother's mother, mother's father, father's mother, father's father, mother's grandmother(s), mother's grandfather(s), father's grandmother(s), father's grandfather(s).

Exploring My Roots

Relative's Name: _____

Relationship to Me: _____

Occupation:

_____

Brothers and/or Sisters:

_____

_____

_____

_____

Children:

_____

_____

_____

Heritage/Nationality:

_____

_____

_____

_____

Any Questions?

When you finished reading *The Hundred Dresses*, did you have any questions that were left unanswered? If so, write them on the lines below.

_____

_____

_____

_____

_____

_____

Next, work in groups to prepare possible answers for some or all of the questions you wrote above and for those written below. After you have finished, share your ideas with the rest of the class.

1. How would you change the end of the story to make things better for everyone?

2. What did the teacher ignore until the principal gave her the letter?

3. What could Peggy have done differently in regards to Wanda?

4. How could Maddie have helped Wanda?

5. Will Wanda have friends at her new school? What will they be like?

6. How do you think this experience will affect Wanda when she tries to meet friends at her next school?

7. Will Wanda's father be able to protect his children from others? Why or why not?

8. What do you think Maddie will do the next time someone new enters her classroom?

9. What lessons might the children have learned since Wanda left?

10. What could the teacher do to help the children become more aware of other cultures?

11. What could the students do to learn more about children from other countries?

12. What would it be like to move to a new country with a different language, money system, and school system?

13. How would you have felt if you were Wanda and the other students teased you every day about your clothing?

14. Name several things that you could do to understand other cultures better.

Book Report Ideas

There are so many ways to report on a book once it has been read. After you have finished reading *The Hundred Dresses*, choose a method of reporting on it that appeals to you. If you have an idea of your own, check it with your teacher first.

Canned Story

This report is made on a long, thin strip of paper. The paper is divided into ten frames (like comic strips). After the divisions are made, each frame will represent an important event which takes place in the story. Each frame should include a short summary explaining the event. The events should be in chronological order. The first frame should include the name of the book and your own name. After the strip is completed and colored, roll it up and place it inside of a can (like an oatmeal container) or a jar. Decorate the outside of the container if you have extra time.

Talk Show

For this type of report you will need to work in a group of three or four. You will be creating a skit in the form of a talk show. The hosts of the talk show can be Maddie, Peggy, and/or Wanda. Other characters (such as Miss Mason, the principal, Mr. Svenson, and the other students in room 13) may be included in the panel. Write a script for your talk show and cover the injustices, feelings, and actions of those people who played a large role or watched the events of the story unfold.

Be a Character

Choose one of the characters from the story and write a narrative from his or her point of view. Cover the main topics of each chapter. Then dress up like the character and present your narrative to the class.

Diorama

Create a diorama representing one of the scenes from the book in a shoebox. Include a summary of the scene and attach it to the back of the box.

Report

Write a one-page summary of the story. Include your feelings about the characters, their choices, and their actions. On a separate piece of paper, draw and color a scene from the story and staple it to the summary.

Pop-up Book

Create a pop-up book with seven pages (one page for each chapter). Include a decorated cover with the name of the book on it. Each pop-up page should include a pop-up from one chapter of the book. Write a two- to three- sentence summary under each pop-up.

Puppet Play

Write a short puppet play (with a group or by yourself) which retells the story. Make your own puppets from socks, paper bags, craft sticks, or any other materials. Present your play to your class.

Drama

With a small group, create a drama that recreates the story. Dress up in costumes and reenact the story.

Research Ideas

Researching and learning about new things can create a broader understanding of our world. Below is a list of ideas to research about *The Hundred Dresses* and the author, Eleanor Estes.

❏ **Country Reports**

Wanda's family came from the country of Poland. Do a research report about Poland or another country that one of your own classmates came from. Find out about the products, population, economy, people, customs, and climate. Make your report two to three pages in length. Add several bonus pages with ideas such as a crossword puzzle or word search of country vocabulary, a map of the country, or a hidden picture puzzle of products or items associated with the country.

❏ **State Reports**

Eleanor Estes was born in Connecticut and later lived in New York. Research one of these two states. Create a two- to three-page report on the state of your choice. Include information about the people, flag, state bird, climate, annual rain and snowfall, population, education, and any other facts which are interesting. Add several bonus pages at the end of your report. Bonus pages might include word searches or crossword puzzles using words associated with the state, hidden picture puzzles showing products of the state, and maps of the state.

❏ **Clothing Design**

Research the career of clothing design. What do clothing designers do? What type of education and preparation do you need to have to become a clothing designer? What personality traits and interests do most clothing designers share? Research the history of clothing design and fashion trends. Include information about some of the most famous designers in history and in our own time. This report should span two to three pages. At the end of your report, add a few sketches of your own original clothing designs. If you can, make some three-dimensional models of your designs out of paper or fabric.

❏ **Gettysburg Address**

Look into the historical context of the Gettysburg Address. When did President Lincoln deliver this speech? What was happening at this point in American history? What was the speech generally about? Why is this speech still so famous today? Rewrite the speech as if it were being delivered today. Use more modern English words and phrases. Your report and speech rewrite should cover two to three pages. After you have written your report, memorize all or part of the Gettysburg Address and recite it to the teacher or the class.

❏ **History of Boats**

Do a research report about the history of boats. What were some of the most primitive boats like? What are some of the most modern boats like? List a few of the most famous boats in history and explain why they are so famous. After writing a research report of two to three pages, create an illustrated time line of boats. Draw sketches of the different types of boats that were used during certain times in history. If you can, make a model (out of materials of your choice) of your favorite type of boat.

Culminating Activities

The Hundred Dresses Wall Mural

Divide the students into seven groups. Assign each group one chapter from the book. Have the groups create a large picture on butcher paper of one or several important events in their assigned chapters. Their murals may include writing or computer printouts. Let them choose the medium they wish to use to communicate the events of the chapter. They may wish to use paints; a mosaic method of paper, fabric pieces, or wallpaper samples; crayons; markers; colored pencils; miscellaneous items such as buttons, string, wire, stickers, sequins, or glitter; or any combination of these.

When the pictures are completed, display them side by side in the classroom or in a school hallway to create one large mural of *The Hundred Dresses*.

Other Lands and People

Choose one day, week, or several time blocks to have a variety of activities to expose your students to other cultures. Below are some activity ideas which encourage students to learn about other lands and cultures.

1. Contact parents with a variety of backgrounds. Ask if they would be willing to give a presentation about their heritage and share such things as food samples, photographs, and souvenirs.

2. Research children's games from other countries. Try them out with your students.

3. Make several art projects that represent different countries. Discuss facts about the countries and cultures as the projects are being created.

4. Share the book *Children Just Like Me* with the class during reading time, discussions, or activities. The students could use the information in the book to keep short journals related to the children listed in the book.

5. Discuss the similarities and differences of people from different cultures and lands. To broaden this experience even further, have your students develop relationships with pen pals from other cultures and lands. Listed below are organizations that may be useful in obtaining pen pals for the students.

Gifted Children's Pen Pals International
c/o Dr. Debby Sue Vandevender
166 E. 61st St.
New York, NY 10021-8509

International Pen Pals
P.O. Box 290065
Brooklyn, NY 11229
Leslie Fox, Regional Rep.

Student Letter Exchange
630 3rd Ave.
New York, NY 10017
Wayne J. Dankert, Gen. Mgr.

World Pen Pals
1694 Como Ave.
St. Paul, MN 55108
Carrie Tahtamouni, Coordinator

Worldwide Friendship International
3749 Brice Run, Suite A
Randallstown, MD 21133
Elton Smith, President

Make A Friend
Children Just Like Me Penpal Club
DK Publishing
95 Madison Ave.
New York, NY 10016

Objective Test and Essay Questions

True or False: Write true or false next to each statement below.

_____1. Maddie is truly sorry about how she treated Wanda.

_____2. Wanda lives in Boggins Heights.

_____3. Peggy is a very selfish girl and never really changes.

Multiple Choice: Choose the letter which is the most correct.

4. Wanda's contest entry is very unusual because . . .

   a. she does a fabulous job.

   b. she does not have any friends.

   c. she eats peanut butter every lunch period.

   d. she enters 100 times.

5. The rumors about Mr. Svenson make Peggy and Maddie feel . . .

   a. happy.

   b. ecstatic.

   c. fearful and scared.

   d. confused.

6. Wanda has a difficult life because . . .

   a. she lives far from the school and has to walk each day.

   b. she has to do her own laundry every evening if she wants clean clothes.

   c. she has no mother to care for her.

   d. none of the children at school are her friends.

   e. only letters a and c

   f. letters a–d

Short Answers: On a separate piece of paper write a short answers for each question.

7. How do Maddie's thoughts about Wanda change from the beginning of the book to the end?

8. Describe Boggins Heights. What is it like to live there?

9. If there was a girl or boy like Wanda in your class, what could you do that would make him or her feel more welcome and needed? What might you learn if you were to give that person a chance?

Paragraphs: Answer one of the following in paragraph form on a separate piece of paper.

10. Write a summary of the book in five or six sentences.

11. Discuss why Maddie does not get more involved in defending Wanda.

12. Suggest some ways to learn more about people who immigrate (to the United States) from other countries.

Explanations and Matching

━━━━━━━━━━━━━━━━━━━━━━ **Explanations** ━━━━━━━━━━━━━━━━━━━━━━

Explain the meaning of each of these quotations from *The Hundred Dresses*.

Chapter 1: . . . "that these dead shall not have died in vain— that this nation shall, under God, have a new birth of freedom— and that government of the people, by the people, for the people, shall not perish from the earth."

Chapter 2: "Wanda, tell us. How many dresses did you say you had hanging up in your closet?"

Chapter 3: ". . . 'October's bright blue weather.'"

Chapter 4: "You'd look like a Christmas tree in that."

Chapter 5a: "I am sure none of my boys and girls in Room 13 would purposely and deliberately hurt anyone's feelings because his name happened to be a long unfamiliar one. I prefer to think that what was said was said in thoughtlessness."

Chapter 5b: "I know that all of you feel the way I do, that this is a very unfortunate thing to have happen. Unfortunate and sad, both. And I want you all to think about it."

Chapter 6: "I never did call her a foreigner or make fun of her name. I never thought she had the sense to know we were making fun of her anyway. I thought she was too dumb."

Chapter 7: "Stop! This girl is just a girl just like you are . . . ."

━━━━━━━━━━━━━━━━━━━━━━ **Matching** ━━━━━━━━━━━━━━━━━━━━━━

Match the names of the characters with their actions and thoughts. Write the matching name next to each sentence.

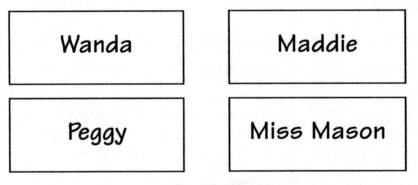

Wanda	Maddie
Peggy	Miss Mason

1. _____ She feels that none of her students would knowingly make fun of others.

2. _____ She dreams many times about being brave and standing up for Wanda.

3. _____ She wears the same blue dress to school every day.

4. _____ She hurts others intentionally and wants to be the most popular person in the class.

Group Pantomimes and Mini-Dramas

Work in size-appropriate groups to perform the following ideas from *The Hundred Dresses*. Each group may choose to act out the ideas silently (pantomime) or to use speech in a dramatization. If pantomiming is used, the ideas must be clearly presented in actions.

1. Wanda, her late arrival to school, and her seat in the classroom (three to five people)

2. the October's bright blue day (five to six people)

3. Maddie and Peggy waiting for Wanda in the rain (two people)

4. Miss Mason receiving the letter and sharing it with the class (four to seven people)

5. the contest, waiting for the results, and the results (four to seven people)

6. Maddie and Peggy talking after the letter and making plans for after school (two people)

7. Maddie and Peggy in Boggins Heights and Wanda's house (two people)

8. seeing old Mr. Svenson and discussing the rumors about him (two to three people)

9. Maddie and her dreams about Wanda (two to three people)

10. writing letters to Wanda (three to four people)

11. Maddie and Peggy going home with their drawings after school (two people)

12. passing around the letter that was received from Wanda (three to five people)

13. Other: _____

_____

_____

Notes for the Performance

_____

_____

Bibliography of Related Reading

Abraham Lincoln

Freedman, Russell. *Lincoln: A Photobiography.* Scholastic, Inc., 1987.

Sandburg, Carl. *Abraham Lincoln.* Harcourt Brace Jovanovich, Inc., 1967.

Strasser, Todd. *Abraham Lincoln for Class President.* Scholastic, Inc., 1995.

Sullivan, George. *Mr. President.* Scholastic, Inc., 1992.

Immigrants

Bukowczyk, John J. *And My Children Did Not Know Me. A History of the Polish-Americans.* Indiana University Press, 1987.

Daniels, Roger. *Coming to America.* HarperCollins Publishers, 1990.

Dinnerstein, Leonard, and David M. Reimers. *Ethnic Americans: A History of Immigration.* Harper and Row, 1987.

Kuniczak, W. S. *My Name Is Million: An Illustrated History of the Poles in America.* Doubleday, 1978.

Moynihan, Daniel Patrick. *The Immigrant Experience.* Chelsea House Publishers, 1989.

Making Friends with Children of Many Nationalities

Kindersley, Barnabas and Anabel. *Children Just Like Me.* Dorling Kindersley, 1995.

Making Friends. Henry Holt and Co. and Raduga Publishers, 1987.

Ships and Boats

Richardson, Joy. *Ships.* Franklin Watts, 1994.

Tunis, Edwin. *Oars, Sails and Steam: A Picture Book of Ships.* World, 1952.

New York

Davis, James E., and Sheryl Davis Hawke. *New York City.* Raintree, 1990.

Connecticut

Fradin, Dennis B. *The Connecticut Colony.* Children's Press, 1994.

Fradin, Dennis B. *From Sea to Shining Sea, Connecticut.* Children's Press, 1990.

Kent, Deborah. *America the Beautiful, Connecticut.* Children's Press, 1989.

Answer Key

Page 11

1. She is quiet, rarely says anything, and cannot read very well. She always wears a faded blue dress, and her shoes are caked with mud.
2. They think she is strange and has a funny name. They tease her.
3. Peggy is popular, always has new clothes, is an excellent artist, and started the game with Wanda.
4. The girls realize Wanda is absent when they wait for her and she does not arrive.
5. She sits in the back, probably to keep to herself or because of her dirty shoes.
6. They are rough and generally misbehaved.
7. The students recite the Gettysburg Address.
8. She is quiet and reserved and never gets into trouble.

Pages 13 and 14

1. candy store
2. Go south on Eucalyptus Lane and then east on Apple Street.
3. Go east on Apple Street and then north on Oak Street.
4. Go south on Oak Street and then west on Apple Street.
5. a. Go north on Oak Street and west on Elm Lane.
   b. Go west on Olive Street and north on Boggins Heights Lane.
6. candy store, restaurant, veterinarian's office, Tom's, Tom's

Page 16

1. They were late.
2. Wanda's desk is dusty, and it looks like she was gone yesterday as well.
3. They play The Hundred Dresses game with Wanda.

They are not paying attention to her feelings. Some of the girls are just following the crowd, and some are just being mean.

4. Wanda tries to fit in by playing along with their game.
5. She stands alone in the schoolyard.
6. She does not like it and feels bad for Wanda. She is also afraid that she will be made fun of next.
7. Answers will vary.
8. Answers will vary.

Page 17

1 small green cabbage, 69¢, $3.45
2 slices of bacon, 20¢, $1.00
1 large onion, chopped, 49¢, $2.45
2 small leeks (white part only), sliced, 50¢, $2.50
2 carrots, sliced, 24¢, $1.20
1 potato, sliced, 50¢, $2.50
1 tablespoon flour, 2¢, 10¢
4 cups of brown stock, 59¢, $2.95
2 tablespoons of parsley, chopped, 40¢, $2.00
1 bay leaf, 10¢, 50¢
a pinch of nutmeg, 2¢, 10¢
1 teaspoon of dill seeds, 30¢, $1.50
4 frankfurters, fried and sliced, 64¢, $3.20
fat for frying, 20¢, $1.00

Total cost = $24.45

Page 18

Yellow/Subject	Green/Predicate
1. Peggy	would (not) stop
2. students	submitted
3. Maddie	sharpened
4. Maddie, Cecile	joined
5. They	stopped, gasped
6. frown	puckered
7. sweaters	caught
8. wind	swished
9. student	did
10. class	applauded
11. Miss Mason	clapped, stomped
12. Bill	shuffled

Page 19

1. Maddie / stumbled on the wet patch of earth.
2. Thoughts of Wanda / floated through her mind slowly.
3. The following day / was extremely drizzly and cold.
4. Many excited students / stared at the colorful dresses.
5. Several light blue clouds / moved gently across the sky.
6. Both boys / burst out laughing loudly.
7. Wanda / silently entered the empty classroom.
8. Maddie's desk / slammed shut with a bang.
9. Big Bill Byron / placed his large, muddy feet on Wanda's chair.
10. Wanda / was absent from school.
11. The two most popular students, Peggy and Maddie, / noticed Wanda was not in school.
12. Several children / chose to color their boats green.

Page 21

1. She keeps thinking about Wanda.
2. It started on a bright October day.
3. She wants to tease Wanda every day. She enjoys teasing Wanda and does not feel bad about it.
4. She wants to fit in.
5. She makes it into a game and begins to tease Wanda.
6. She describes the colors of the dresses and acts as if her story is true.
7. All of the children who are around.
8. She was happy and joyful. The weather was beautiful. She found a broken mirror and the sun hit it. It reflected on Wanda, and even she looked pretty.

Answer Key *(cont.)*

Page 22

1. 20 days
2. 30 days
3. 224 students
4. 64 pencils
5. 6 desks
6. 96 pieces of paper
7. 64 designs
8. $16.00 total
9. 160 glances
10. 50 blocks

Page 25

1. She wants to write a note to ask Peggy to stop playing the game. However, she worries that Peggy might start teasing her too.
2. Boys have to draw motorboats.
3. Girls have to draw dresses.
4. Maddie thinks Peggy will win.
5. She forgets about Wanda.
6. She has not learned English very well yet, or she has reading problems.
7. They do not want to be teased also.
8. She is the most popular girl in the class.

Page 27

Adjectives	Adverbs
1. tiny	slowly
2. happy	curiously
3. Silly	quietly
4. Grumpy	angrily
5. excited	wildly, loudly
6. Seven	noisily
7. Rambunctious	breathlessly
8. Young	neatly
9. kind	patiently
10. Old	fast, hard
11. Wise	sadly
12. thoughtless	carelessly

Page 30

1. It is raining, and they do not want to be late.

2. Wanda wins the contest. She enters 100 times.
3. Miss Mason is sad and upset. She hopes that none of her students would purposely harm or tease others, and she asks them to think about what happened.
4. Maddie feels horrible.
5. Peggy often asked Wanda how many dresses she had.
6. There are so many entries and not enough space.
7. She does not stick up for Wanda; she just lets the game continue.
8. She says, "Hey, let's go and see if that kid has left town or not."

Page 31

a dress

Page 32

a boat

Page 35

1. Boggins Heights is drab, cold, and cheerless.
2. They heard that he had shot a man.
3. It is a little white house with chicken coops. The house and yard are shabby but clean.
4. They feel disappointed and discouraged.
5. They do not have Wanda's new address, and there is no forwarding address. They hope that the post office will forward it.
6. She sticks up for Wanda no matter what.
7. She says it to try to fit in with the other girls.
8. Wanda might have really liked them. The picture looks like her.

Bonus answers will vary.

Page 36

1. bad living conditions, lack of jobs, prejudice, poor housing, crowded neighborhoods, unsanitary living conditions
2. Immigrants today often need to learn a new language, new customs, and a different currency system (among many other things).
3. Accept all reasonable answers.
4. They have their students wear uniforms.
5. Accept all uniform designs.

Page 43

1. True
2. True
3. True
4. d
5. c
6. f
7. She realizes that Wanda is a girl like herself with feelings, too.
8. In the summer Boggins Heights has wild flowers and a flowing brook. In the fall it is dismal and cheerless, and it is cluttered with trash.
9. Accept all reasonable answers.
10. Accept all reasonable answers.
11. Accept all reasonable answers.
12. Accept all reasonable answers.

Page 44

Accept all reasonable answers.
1. Miss Mason
2. Maddie
3. Wanda
4. Peggy

Page 45

Accept all reasonable skits.